Mission Statement
for...

Safari as a Way of Life.

" To explore the unknown and the familiar, distant and near, and to record in detail with the eyes of a child, any beauty, (of the flesh or otherwise) horror, irony, traces of utopia or Hell. Select your team with care, but when in doubt, take on ^some new crew and give them a chance. But avoid at all costs fluctuations of sincerity with your best people. "

"find Clarity of Vision"

Dan Eldon

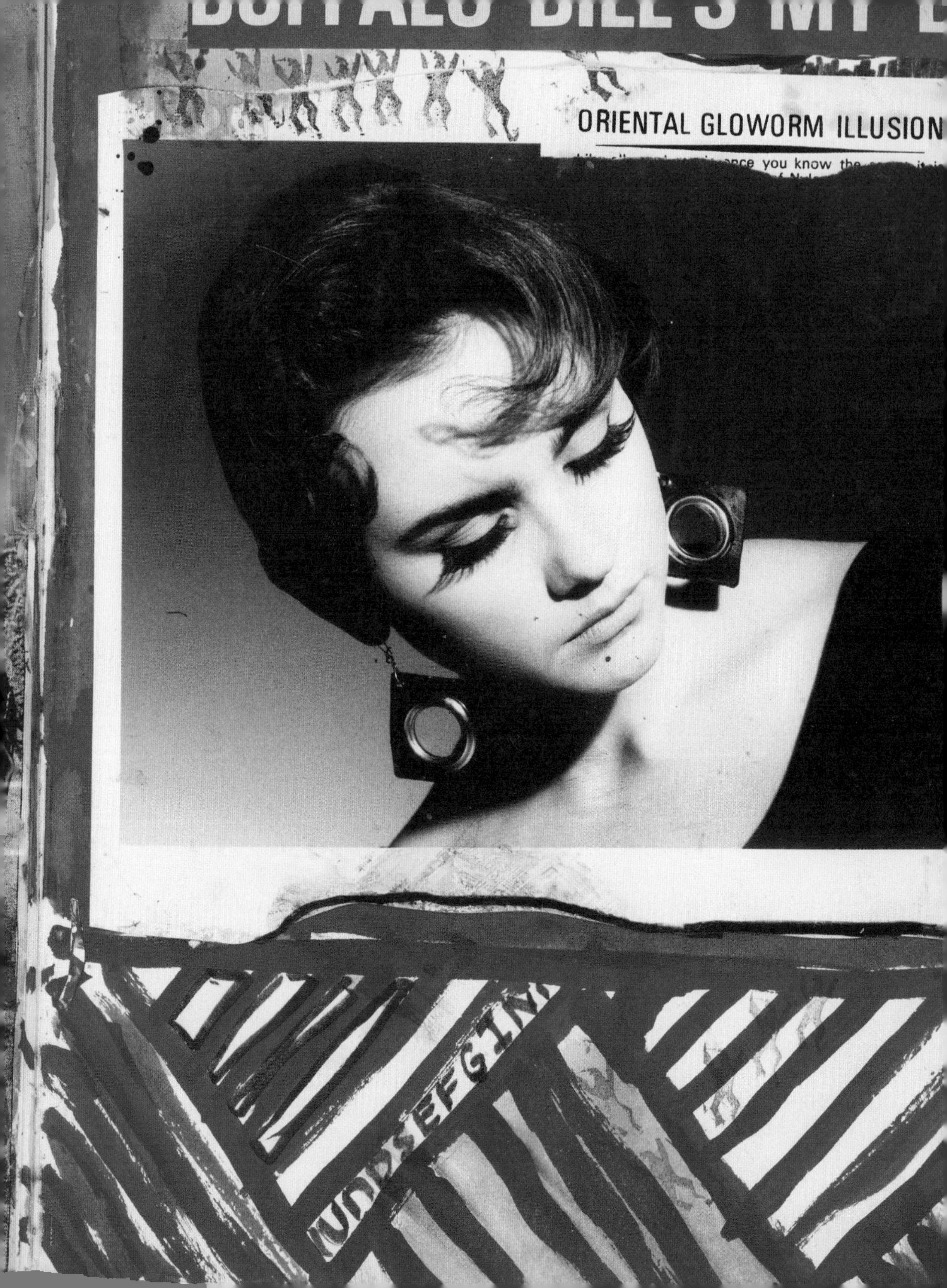
ORIENTAL GLOWORM ILLUSION

There is little difference between being lost and exploring.

The most important part of vehicle maintenance is clean windows so if you are broken down, you will enjoy the beauty of the view.

It's better to go somewhere than not to.

~ look for solutions ~ not problems. ~

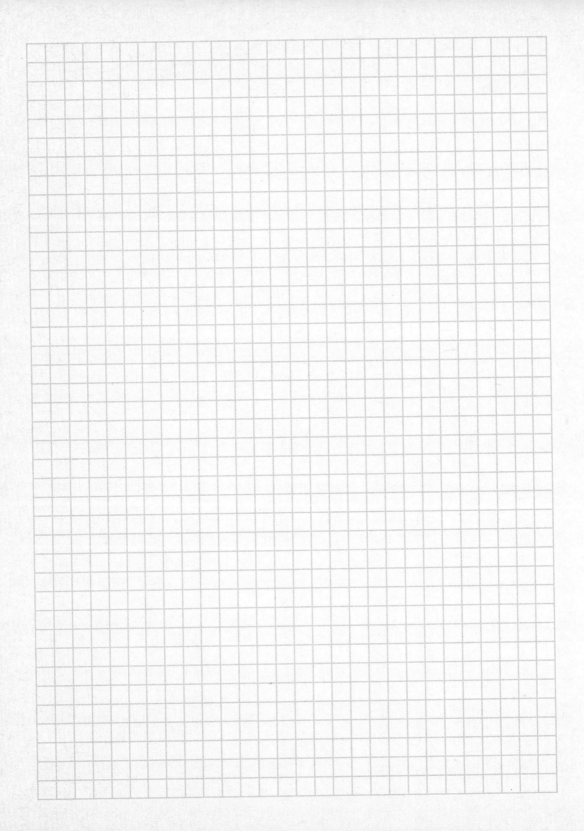

"find clarity of Vision"

Now is the best time to live.

"The Journey is the Destination..." Dan Eldon

Safari as a Way of Life.

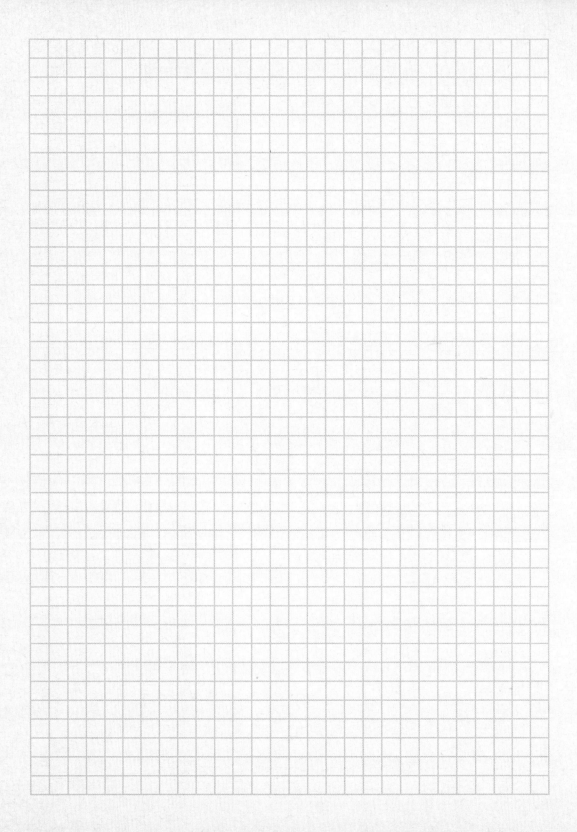

In general, life is good.

In specific, it is excellent.

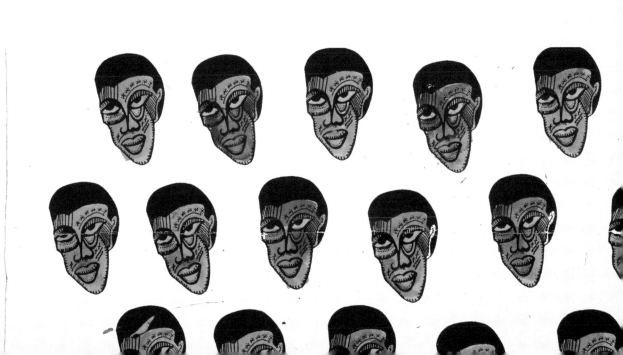

Tanzania,
Mikumi
Nat. Park.

The illegal campsite in Mikumi National Park. The next morning, we busted
out through a newly made road. Made in fact by Dr. Croze and F...

Dedicated to all those who lost their lives during the drama...

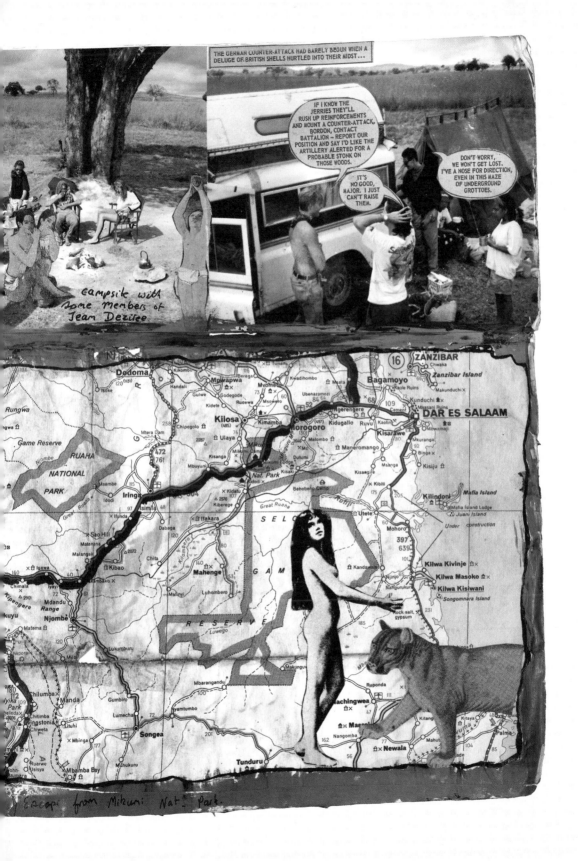

campsite with some Members of Jean Deziree.

Escape from Mikumi Nat. Park.

It's better to go somewhere than not to.

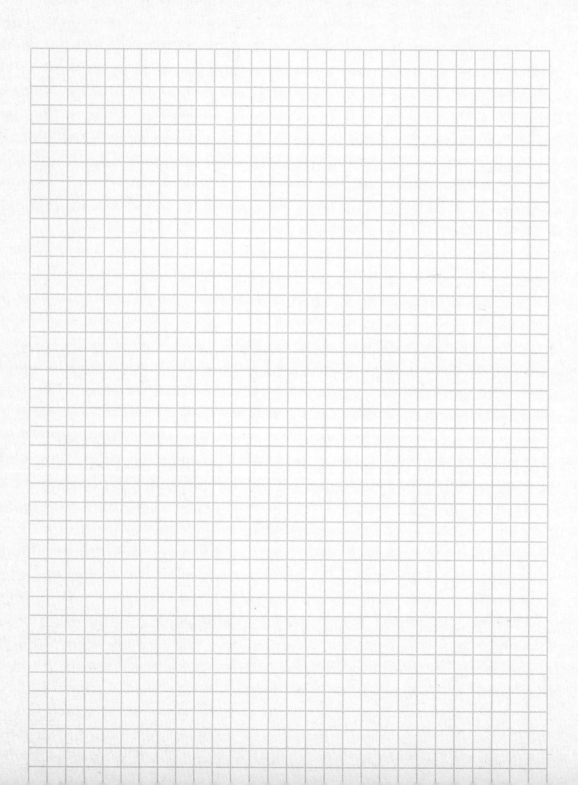

free at last...

"The Journey is the Destination..." Dan Eldon

Safari as a Way of Life.

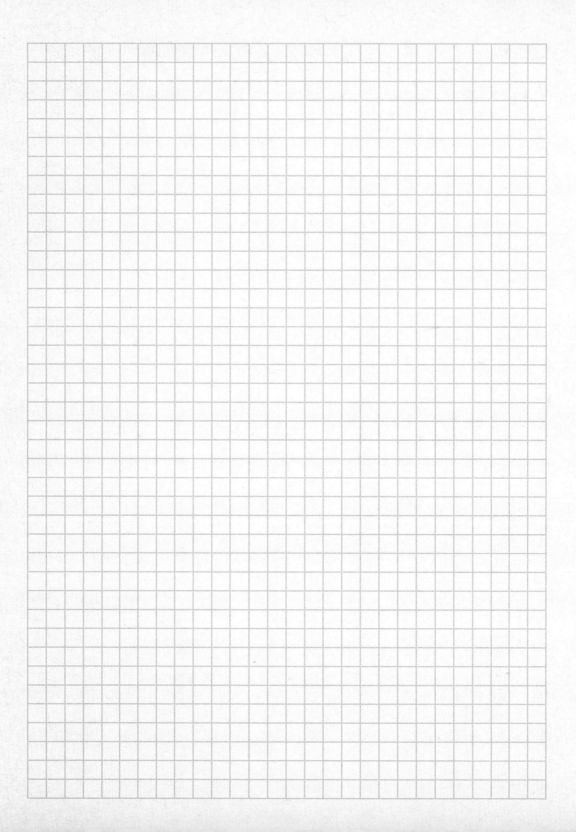

In general, life is good.

In specific, it is excellent.

"find clarity of Vision"

Dan Eldon

HISTORY OF MY FACE
1981 — 1991

FILM FOR COLOR SLIDES
Kodachrome
200
L 135-36
36 EXP
DX 35 mm

Kodak
Gold
FOR COLOR PRINTS
5-24
4 EXP 100

Gold
FILM FOR COLOR PRINTS
135-24
4 EXP 100

ILFORD
XP2
400
DX 135 36

Kodak
Gold
FILM FOR COLOR PRINTS
GA 135-36
36 EXP

Kodak
EKTAR
1000
35mm
CJ 135-24
R COLOUR PRINTS
UR ÉPREUVES COULEUR

Gold
FILM FOR COLOR PRINTS
GA 135-24
24 EXP 100

ILFORD
XP2
400
DX 135 36

Kodak
EKTAR
1000
35mm
CJ 135-24

Gold
FILM FOR COLOR PRINT

ILFORD
XP2
400

135-36
NEOPAN
1600

There is little difference between being lost and exploring.

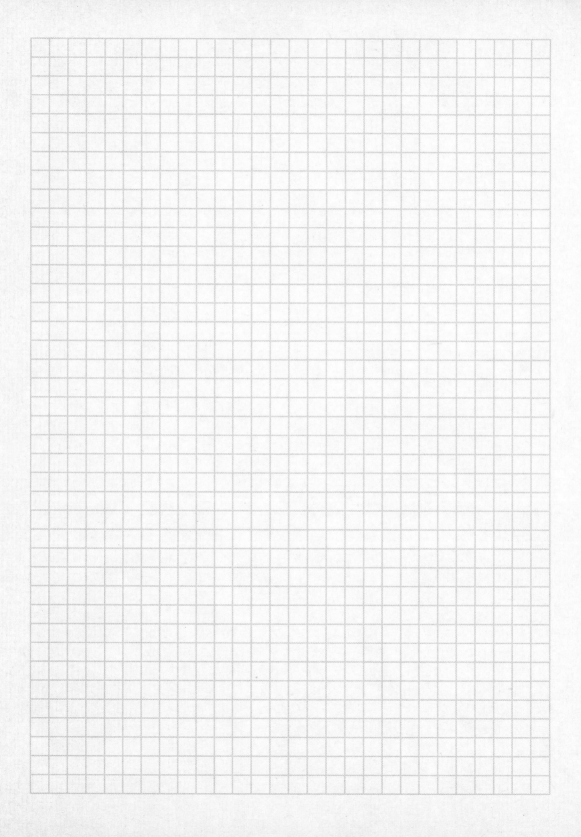

It's better to go somewhere than not to.

LONDON UNDERGROUND ⊖ LONDON UNDERGROUND ⊖ LONDON UNDERGROUND ⊖ LONDON UN

OXFORD CIRCUS

~ look for solutions - not problems. ~

Now is the best time to live.

SINCERITY
SAFARI
SAFARI AS A WAY OF LIFE!
THE BIG ONE
18
18

EIGHTEEN

Safari as a Way of Life.

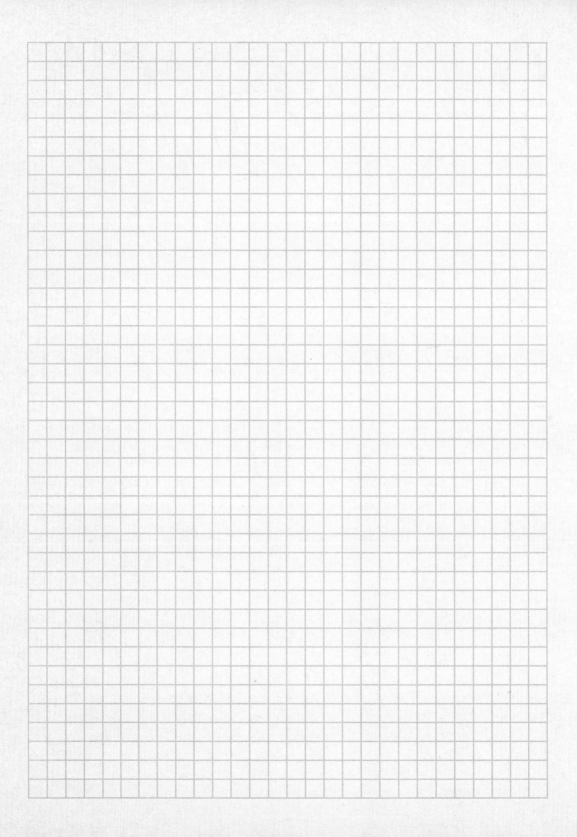

"The Journey is the Destination..." Dan Eldon

In general, life is good.

In specific, it is excellent.

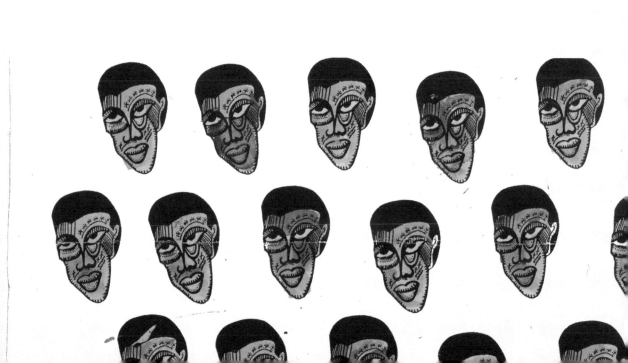